A JOURNEY
INTO
SERENITY

A JOURNEY INTO SERENITY

A PERSONAL PATH TO SELF-TRANSFORMATION

SUSAN FLYNN

Xulon Press

Xulon Press
2301 Lucien Way #415
Maitland, FL 32751
407.339.4217
www.xulonpress.com

Paperback ISBN-13: 978-1-66285-345-6
Ebook ISBN-13: 978-1-66285-346-3

DEDICATION

To my two amazing children Damian and Logan—may your journey in this life be epic.

First, I would like to thank GOD, my family, and some of the most amazing people in my life. I feel blessed to have met you on this journey!

This manuscript is my gift of love to you, my readers!

INTRODUCTION

MY INTENTION FOR this book is to help you to begin a journey of discovering treasures within yourself and to assist as you plumb the depth of the strength and beauty within you. Having done that, you can embark on the journey to dominate and achieve mastery of your soul and, hence, your life.

One very optimal way is learning to manage your emotions and have them serve you. Too many people live in constant stress of being perturbed, agitated, angry, and upset. My intention is to assist you as you open your eyes to a new reality that is possible and a space of happiness as you grow in becoming more aware of the power of the resources within you so you can become the boss.

I have been reading and collecting these beautifully philosophic quotes for over twenty five years. I started to collect these quotes when a friend gifted me this little book and encouraged me to read it. I asked myself, "What is this little book going to do for me anyways?" I did not realize at that time that it was a seed toward my transformation. Your life will begin to shift as you allow these words to inspire you.

WHO AM I?
WHERE DID I COME FROM?

1- An old Cherokee story about these dilemmas which all of us agonize over.

"An elder tells his grandson, every choice in life is a battle between two wolves inside us. One represents anger, envy, greed, fear. Lies, insecurities, and ego. The others represent peace, love, compassion. Kindness, humility, and positivity. They are competing for supremacy: which wolf wins you may ask? The one you feed."

- Unknown

2- The Train of Life: Life is like a journey on a train: with its stations, with changes of routes, and with accidents! At birth, we boarded the train and met our parents, and we believed they would always travel on our side; however, at some stations, our parents would step down from the train, leaving us on this journey alone.

As time goes by, other people will board the train, and they will be significant, like our siblings, friends, children, and even the love of our life, and they may step down and leave a permanent vacuum.

Others will go so unnoticed that we don't realize that they vacated their seats, which is very sad when you think about it. This train ride will be full of joy, sorrow, fantasy, expectations, hellos, goodbyes, and farewells. Success consists of having a good relationship with all the passengers, requiring that we give the best of ourselves.

The mystery to everyone is: we don't know at which station we ourselves will step down. So, we must live in the best way, love, forgive, and offer the best of who we are. It is important to do that because when the time comes for us to step down and leave our seats empty, we should leave behind beautiful memories for those who will continue to travel on the train of life. I wish you a joyful journey this year on the train of life. Reap success and give lots of love. More importantly, give thanks for the journey. Lastly, I thank you for being one of the passengers of my train!

- Unknown

3- When people walk away from you, let them go. Your destiny is never tied to anyone who leaves you. And it doesn't mean they are bad people. It just means that their part in your story is over.

- Tony McCollum

4- When the universe is making you wait, and it feels like you've been forgotten, be prepared because you are going to receive so much more than you asked for.

- Susan Flynn

5- In this world, we are all sick, so don't judge someone with a different disease. No one is perfect; you are most certainly not perfect.

- Susan Flynn

6- Hate no one, even if they've wronged you. Stay humble, no matter how much wealth you encounter. Be positive, no matter how hard life gets. Forgive always, especially yourself. And never stop seeing the best in people.

- Susan Flynn

7- I stand for honesty, equality, kindness, compassion, treating people the way you want to be treated, and helping those in need. To me, those are traditional values.

- Ellen DeGeneres

8- The appearance of things changes according to the emotions, and thus we see magic and beauty in them, while the magic and beauty are really in ourselves.

- Kahlil Gibran

9- Motivation: This is what gets you started. Habit is what keeps you going.

- Jim Rohn

10- A loving heart is always healthy. A serving heart is always happy. A caring heart is always strong. And I pray God keeps you healthy, happy, and strong always.

- Susan Flynn

11- Sometimes the best thing to do for yourself is nothing—not wonder, not think, not obsess, just breathe, and remember everything works out for the best. Gandhi said you find yourself when you lose yourself in the services of others.

- Susan Flynn

12- Don't ever be impressed with goal setting; be impressed with goal getting. Reaching new goals and moving to a higher level of performance always requires change, and change feels awkward.

But take comfort in the knowledge that if change doesn't feel uncomfortable, then it's probably not really a change.

- John Maxwell

13- Decide what you want in your life. Believe you will get it with every fiber of your being. Live as if you already have it, feel it to be yours, and it soon will be yours.

- Susan Flynn

14- Detachment is not that you own nothing. Detachment is that nothing owns you.

- Bhagavad Gita

15- Take care of your mind, your body, and your soul because you only have control over these three things in your life—the thoughts you think, the images you visualize, and the actions you take.

- Susan Flynn

16- There are five types of affiliations in this life: you must have all five—physical, financial, mental, emotional, and spiritual—for a well-balanced life.

- Susan Flynn

17- PEACE: It does not mean to be in a place where there is no noise, trouble, or hard work. It means to be in the midst of those things and still be calm in your heart.

- Buddha

18- Surround yourself with people who will take care of you not materialistically, but take care of your soul, your heart, and everything that is you.

- Susan Flynn

19 Sow a thought, reap an action. Sow an action, reap a habit. Sow a habit, reap a character. Sow a character, reap a destiny.

- Ralph Waldo Emerson

20- We should plant trees under whose shade we do not plan to sit.
- Bhagavad Gita

21- Being a candle is not easy. To give light, one must burn.

- Rumi

22- No matter how deep the issue is and no matter how long you have struggled with it, the possibility exists for you to become absolutely free, whole, and healed.

- Brandon Bay

23- A frog decided he was going to reach the top of the tree. All the other frogs shouted, "It's impossible, it's impossible!" but, the frog reaches the top. How, may you ask? He was deaf, and he thought everyone was shouting you can do it, you can do it, Moral of the story—be deaf to negative thoughts and words and aim to reach your goal.

- Susan Flynn

24- Permanence and persistence in spite of all obstacles, discouragements, and impossibilities: it is this that in all things distinguishes the strong soul from the weak.

- Thomas Carlyle

TRUE STORY

25- There was a king, one of the richest kings in the world. He had money, gold, diamonds, land, and places, more than anyone could imagine. The king got sick; his men had the best doctors from all over the world, trying to make him better. No one could. His doctors asked him, "Do you have any last wishes?"

He said, "Yes, when I die, I want all the best doctors to carry my coffin. Let them lay all the gold, diamonds, and money on the ground where my coffin is laid for viewing. I want the coffin to be open with my hands out."

"Why?" they asked.

"I want the world to see that all the greatest doctors in the world nor all the wealth couldn't save me. I came to this world empty-handed, and I'm leaving this world empty-handed."

- Unknown

26- Show respect to people even when they don't deserve it. Respect is a reflection of your character, not theirs.

- Susan Flynn

27- You must be the change you wish to see in the world.

- Gandhi

28- Nothing is permanent in this world, not even our troubles.

- Charlie Chaplin.

29- I believe that everything happens for a reason. People change so that you can learn to let go, things go wrong so that you appreciate them when they're right, you believe lies so you eventually learn to trust no one but yourself, and sometimes good things fall apart so better things can fall together.

- Marilyn Monroe

30- Circumstances do not make a man—they reveal him.

- James Alle

31- Caring about what people think of you is useless. Most people don't even know what they think of themselves. Just focus on becoming a better you everyday.

- Susan Flynn

32- Before you argue with someone, ask yourself, is that person even mentally mature enough to grasp the concept of a different perspective? Because if not, there's absolutely no point.

- Tiny Buddha

33- Be like a tree. Stay grounded. Connect with your roots. Turn over a new leaf. Bend before you break. Enjoy your unique natural beauty. Keep growing.

- Susan Colton

34- The main purpose of life is to live rightly, think rightly, act rightly; the soul languishes when we give all our thought to the body.

- Gandhi

35- When you are happy, you enjoy the music, but when you're sad, you understand the lyrics.

- Jay Shetty

36- I am different, and it has cost me many people, but I'm always myself.

It is better to lose others than to lose yourself while trying to please others. Always stay true to yourself and what you believe in.

- Susan Flynn

37- You must not lose faith in humanity. Humanity is an ocean; if a few drops of water from the ocean are dirty, the ocean does not become dirty.

- Gandhi

38- Keep your face always towards the sunshine and shadows will fall behind you.

- Walt Whitman

39- Spread love everywhere you go. Let no one ever come to you without leaving happier.

- Mother Teresa

40- There are two ways to be fooled. One is to believe what isn't true; the other is to refuse to believe what is true.

- Soren Kierkegaard

41- A healthy discontent is a prelude to progress. Live as if you were to die tomorrow. Learn as if you were to live forever.

- Gandhi

42- Don't let anyone walk through your mind with their dirty feet. An honest disagreement is often a sign of progress.

- Gandhi

43- AN INDIAN PRAYER.

O, great spirit, whose voice I heard in the wind and whose breath gave life to all the world, hear me; I am small and weak; I need your strength, your hand, and your wisdom. Let me walk in beauty and make my eyes ever behold the red and purple sunset. Make my hands to respect the things you have made and my ears sharp to hear your voice. Make me wise so that I may understand the things you have taught my people. Let me learn the lessons you have hidden in every leaf and rock.

Let me seek strength, not to be greater than my brother but to fight my greatest enemy–myself. Make me always ready to come to you with clean hands and straight eyes so when life fades as the fading sunset, my spirit may come to you without shame.

- Chief Yellow Lark

44- Be your own best friend, love yourself, fight for yourself, take care of yourself, make yourself happy, never give up on your dreams, dream big, and chase after them.

- Susan Flynn

45- On this journey, this woman has cheated death, fought thousands of battles and is still standing, has cried a thousand tears and is still smiling. She has been broken, betrayed, abandoned, rejected, but she still walks proud, laughs loud, lives without fear, loves without doubt. This woman is beautiful; this woman is humble; this woman is strong. THIS WOMAN IS ME!

- Susan Flynn

46- The successful man will profit from his mistakes and try again in a different way.

- Dale Carnegie

47- Lord, make me an instrument of thy peace. Where there is hatred, let me sow love.

- Saint Francis

48- Stop letting people who do so little for you control so much of your mind, feelings, and emotions.

- Will Smith

49- To make a difference in someone's world, you don't have to be amazing, rich, talented, beautiful, or perfect. You just have to be you and care.

- Rebecca Fox

50- The sun doesn't wake up thinking how it's going to shine, but it brightens the whole world; we should be like the sun and just shine.

- Susan Flynn

51- As I get older, I am becoming more selective of who I let into my life. I would rather have four quarters than a thousand pieces.

- Susan Flynn

52- When you are tempted to react, stop and ask yourself this question: "Do I want to be a prisoner of my past.?"

- Susan Flynn

53- **Dance:** As though no one is watching.
Love: As though you have never been hurt before.
Sing: As though no one can hear you.
Live: As though heaven is on earth.

- Souza

54- When you learn little, you feel you know a lot, but when you learn a lot, you realize you know very little.

- Jay Shetty

55- I'm not perfect. I've made some bad decisions and wrong choices. I've said the wrong things; I've said the right things. I don't like everything I've done, but I did it because I'm me. I've loved and trusted the wrong people. If I had a chance to start again, I wouldn't change a thing. Why? Because I'm me. There are a lot of good things about me; you just need to look past my imperfections.

- Susan Flynn

56- When you arise in the morning, think of what a precious privilege it is to be alive, to breathe, to think, to enjoy, to love.

- Marcus Aurelius

57- The happiness of your life depends upon the quality of your thoughts. If you learn to control your mind, you control your thoughts; only then will you find real happiness.

- Susan Flynn

58- Discovery consists of seeing what everybody has seen and thinking what nobody has thought.

- Albert Szent

59- Our purpose in this life is to help others. And if you can't help them, don't hurt them. When we learn to give from our heart, then we'll find happiness.

- Susan Flynn

60- Don't change who you are to win someone's approval. Always be authentic stay true to yourself, and you'll find someone who is going to like you for being you because you are special.

- Susan Flynn

61- Love someone not because they give you what you need but because they give you feelings you never thought you needed.

- Unknown

62- Don't hold onto negative feelings by justifying why you are right and someone else is wrong.

- Deepak Chopra

63- I've missed more than 9,000 shots in my career. I've lost almost 300 games. Twenty-six times I've been trusted to take the game's winning shot and missed. I've failed over and over again in my life, and that is why I succeed.

- Michael Jordan

64- Kindness is helping someone in their time of need by giving your strength. Instead of reminding them of their weakness, be kind to everyone.

- Susan Flynn

65- Instead of buying your children all the things you never had, you should teach them all the things you were never taught. Material things wear out; knowledge stays.

- Bruce Lee

66- Never complain about what you don't have; always be grateful for what you do have.

- Susan Flynn

67- Your attitude is like a price tag; it shows how valuable you are. When someone does something wrong, don't forget all the things they did right for no one is perfect.

- Susan Flynn

68- Dead people receive more flowers than the living ones because regrets are stronger than gratitude.

-Anne Frank

69- Happiness is a choice. Nothing and no one can make you happy until you choose to do so because happiness comes from within.

- Susan Flynn

70- Negative people deplete your energy. Surround yourself with love and nourishment and do not allow the creation of negativity in your environment.

- Deepak Chopra

71- You only fail when you stop trying. If your dreams don't scare you, they aren't big enough.

- Sir Richard Branson

72- Don't give away your power. We have the power to choose, the power to forgive, the power to love, the power to overcome anything, but when we blame others, we give away our power to them.

- Susan Flynn

73- A beautiful day begins with a great mindset. When you wake up take a moment to think about what a privilege it is to simply be alive and healthy. The moment you start acting like life is a blessing, it becomes a blessing.

- Susan Flynn

74- You must let go of the wrong people in your life to make room for the right ones.

- Susan Flynn

75- People say a lot, so watch what they do because action speaks louder than words.

- Susan Flynn

76- Have the courage to break the patterns that are no longer a service to your life.

- Susan Flynn

77- Always remember in the midst of difficulties lies opportunity.
- Susan Flynn

78- Sometimes the strongest among us are the ones who smile through silent pain, cry behind closed doors and fight battles nobody knows about.

- Zig Ziglar

79- When you truly care for someone, their mistakes never change your feelings because it's the mind that gets angry, but the heart still cares.

- Buddha

80- Nobody has it easy; everyone has issues. You never know what people are going through, so before you start judging or criticizing someone, pause and ask yourself, what battle might this person be fighting?

- Susan Flynn

81- Train your mind to see the good in every situation. You have two choices: to control your mind or let your mind control you.

- Paulo Coelho

82- Never say sorry for telling the truth; nothing will bring you greater peace than doing what is right.

- Susan Flynn

83- Be mindful of who you let into your life. The wrong people will find you in peace and leave you in pieces, but the right people will find you in pieces and lead you into peace.

- Susan Flynn

84- If someone disrespects you or treats you badly, just remember, it is not your fault you did nothing wrong. There is something wrong with them, and that is their way of asking for help. Just remember healthy people do not go around disrespecting other people.

- Susan Flynn

85 -I heard my mom asking our neighbor for some salt. We had salt at home, so I asked her why she was asking. She told me, "They don't have much money, and they sometimes ask us for things, so I asked for something small that wouldn't burden them. I wanted them to feel as if we needed them too. That way, it will be much easier for them to ask us for anything they need."

- Unknown

86- After you let go of enough ego, you naturally feel the peace and joy of yourself.

- Lester Levenson

87- Learn to love yourself, because that's who you will be spending the rest of your life with.

- Susan Flynn

88- If one dream should fall and break into a thousand pieces, never be afraid to pick one of those pieces up and begin again.

- Flavia Weedn

89- Integrity is doing the right thing even when no one is watching.

- C.S. Lewis

90- I'm just a human being trying to make it in a world that is very rapidly losing its understanding of being human.

- John Trudell

91- When you try to control everything, you enjoy nothing. Just relax, breathe, and live in the moment because this moment is all you have.

- Susan Flynn

92- Regrets will not change your past, Anxiety will not change your future, but being greatful will absolutely change your Present.
- Susan Flynn

93- If you truly believe in yourself, anything is possible.
- Susan Flynn

94- Life is about balance. Be kind, but don't let people abuse you. Trust, but don't get deceived. Be content, but never stop improving yourself.
- Zig Ziglar

95- Happiness doesn't depend on what we have, but it does depend on how we feel about what we have. We can be happy with little and miserable with much.
- William D Hoard

96- I am a lover of what is, not because I'm a spiritual person but because I hurt when I argue with reality.
- Bryon Katie

97- When someone is ignoring you, they're teaching you to live without them.
- Susan Flynn

98- The most beautiful things in life are not things. They are the people, places, feelings, moments, smiles, and laughter we enjoy.
- Susan Flynn

99- Anything which is troubling you, anything which is irritating you, that is your teacher.

-Ajahn Chah

100- YOU didn't get to where you are today for nothing. Remember, there is a purpose for every challenge, a lesson for every mistake, and an accomplishment for every step you take. Life isn't easy, and everything happens for a reason, so keep moving forward, and most importantly, never give up.

- Roger Lee

101- We all have negative thoughts; we must not allow those thoughts to control us. Stay positive always.

- Susan Flynn

102- The happiest people I know are always evaluating themselves. The unhappy people are usually evaluating and judging others.

- Lisa Villa Prosen

103- In times of pain, confusion, sorrow, anger, and fear, go within; trust your heart and let it be your guide from any storm. No one can bring you peace but yourself. Everything we're looking for outside is already within us.

- Susan Flynn

104- When we learn acceptance instead of expectance, we will have fewer disappointments.

- Susan Flynn

105- We all fight through some challenging days to get to the best days of our lives.

- Susan Flynn

106- To love and be loved is just amazing. Always listen to your heart. It may be on the left, however, it's always right. Love doesn't need to be perfect; it just needs to be.

- Susan Flynn

107- Live every day to the fullest. Cherish every moment and everyone for you never know when it will be that last time you see someone. Life is fragile; take nothing and no one for granted.

- Susan Flynn

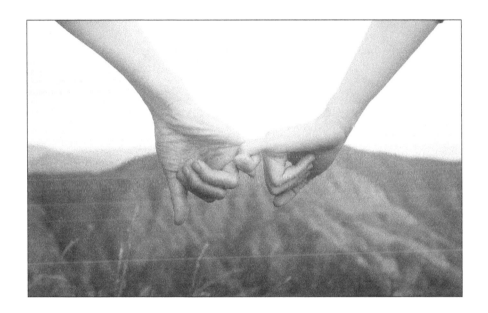

108- If you give ten people the same ingredients and ask them to make a meal, do you think all ten meals will taste the same? So, we are all humans, and we are all the same yet different.

- Susan Flynn

109- One day, all of us will get separated from each other. We will miss our conversations; days, months, and years will pass until our contact becomes rare. One day, our children will see our photo and ask, "Who are these people?" And we will smile with invisible tears and say, "It was with them I had the days of my life."

-Rehman Khan

110- Ignorance is compared to a dangerous body of water, and transcendental knowledge to the boat that can safely carry one across.

- Bhagavad Gita

111- Let us always meet each other with a smile for the smile is the beginning of a great friendship, a smile can change someone's life.

- Susan Flynn

112- Not all of us can do great things. But we can do small things with great love.

- Mother Teresa

113- Kind words can be short and easy to speak, but their echoes are truly endless.

-Mother Teresa

114- Holding on to anger is like grasping a hot coal with the intent of throwing it at someone else; you are the one who gets burned.

- Buddha

115- Being unwanted, unloved, uncared for, forgotten by every-one—I think that is a much greater hunger, a much greater poverty than the person who has nothing to eat.

- Mother Teresa

116- If we have no peace, it's because we have forgotten we belong to each other.

- Mother Teresa

117- As we express our gratitude, we must never forget that the highest appreciation is not utter words, but to live by them.

- John F Kennedy

118- It's not the magnitude of your actions, but the amount of love that is put into them that matters.

- Mother Teresa

119- I can do things you cannot; you can do things I cannot; together, we can do great things.

- Mother Teresa

120- Being rude is easy. It does not take any effort and is a sign of weakness and insecurity. Kindness shows great self-esteem. Being kind is not always easy when dealing with rude people. Kindness is a sign of a person who has done a lot of personal work and has come to a great self-understanding and wisdom. Choose to be kind over being right, and you'll be right every time because kindness is a sign of strength.

- Amanda Rose

121- Inquire submissively and render service unto such a person; the self-realized souls can impart knowledge into you because they have seen the truth.

- Bhagavad Gita

122- Within each living thing, a soul resides, equal inequality to all others. All living beings are equal.

- Bhagavad Gita

123- Life doesn't allow for us to go back and fix what we have done wrong in the past, but it does allow us to live each day better than our last.

- Tiny Buddha

124- I no longer apologize for:

1-My feelings
2-Having boundaries
3-Saying no
4-Being sad
5-Not answering my phone
6-Taking a break
7-Speaking the truth
8-Other people's behavior
9-Becoming a better me
10-Not agreeing
11-Putting myself first
12- Healing at my own pace
13-Not settling.

- Susan Flynn

125- The way I see it, if you want the rainbow, you gotta put up with the rain.

- Dolly Parton

126- Don't let life discourage you. Everyone who got to where he had to had begun where he was.

- Richard L. Eve

127-Live your dream. Do what you love. Cherish every moment. Be brave. Take risks. Create your own happiness. Have an open mind and heart. Make a real difference. Never give up. Dream big. Be fearless. Make every moment count. Today is the day.

- Rebekka Redd- fly fisher

128- I've seen better days, but I have also seen worse. I don't have everything that I want, but I do have all I need. I woke up with the same aches and pains, but I woke up; my life may not be perfect, but I'm blessed.

- Buddha

129- Don't downgrade your dreams to just fit your reality; upgrade your conviction to match your destiny.

- Stuart Scott

130- A loveless world is a dead world. Don't walk behind me; I may not lead. Don't walk in front of me; I may not follow. Just walk beside me and be my friend. Read. Generosity towards the future lies in giving all to the present, but in the end, one needs more courage to live than to kill himself. You will never be happy if you continue to search for what happiness consists of; you will never live if you are looking for the meaning of life. To be happy, we must not be too concerned with things in order to know ourselves. Autumn is the second spring when every leaf is a flower.

- Albert Camus

131- Do not mind anything that anyone tells you about anyone else. Judge everyone and everything for yourself.

- Henry James

132- The secret of change is to focus all of your energy not on fighting the old, but on building the new.

- Mark Twain

133- Life is like a camera. Just focus on what's important and capture the good times, develop from the negative, and if things don't work out, just take another shot.

- Ziad K. Abdelnour

134- The happiness one gets from society, friendship, and love is like a drop of water in the desert. In the west desert, one drop of water is insignificant; it cannot satisfy one's innermost desire for spiritual pleasure.

- Bhagavad Gita

135- When someone dies and we all gather at the funeral, we often reflect. One day, our bodies will also be burnt to ashes or buried. Why are we working so hard? What is the use of it at all? With these thoughts, we become renounced, but because we are influenced by material desires born of ignorance, we quickly forget.

- Susan Flynn

136- If someone tells you it can't be done, it's a reflection of their limitation, not yours. Anything is possible once you put your mind to it.

- Susan Flynn

137- I can teach anybody how to get what they want out of life; the problem is, I can't find anybody who can tell me what they want.
- Mark Twain

138- Wisdom is the reward you get for a lifetime of listening when you'd have preferred to talk.

- Doug Larson

139- Anger is an acid that can do more harm to the vessel in which it is stored than to anything in which it's poured.

- Mark Twain

140-Have a heart that never hardens, a temper that never tires, and a touch that never hurts.

- Charles Dickens

141- There is nothing so strong or safe in an emergency of life as the simple truth.

- Charles Dickens

142- Real friendship is shown in times of trouble; prosperity is full of friends.

- Euripides

143- The peace you are seeking is already present. That peace is seemingly obscure because our attention is being diverted into thinking.

- Kalyani Lawry

144- I am not everything that happened to me. I am everything I became while I healed—stronger but softer, focused but not obsessed, a teacher but still a student. I am not broken. I am beautiful. I am a survivor.

- Buddha

145- There are only two days in the year that nothing can be done. One is called yesterday, and the other is called tomorrow, so today is the right to love, believe, do, and, mostly, live.

- Dalai Lama

146- Whoso neglects to learn in his youth, loses the past and is dead for the future.

- Euripides

147- The worst people to be around are the ones who complain about everything and appreciate nothing.
Surround yourself with {OQP}—only quality people.

- Susan Flynn

148- Today is the tomorrow you worried about yesterday. The tragedy isn't getting something or failing to get it; it's losing something you already have wasted on fresh tears over old griefs.

- Euripides

149- The best and the safest thing is to keep balance in your life. Acknowledge the great power around us and in us. If you can do that and live that way, you are a wise man.

- Euripides

150- We must take care of our minds because we cannot benefit from beauty when our brains are missing.

- Euripides

151- You must tell yourself, "No matter how hard it is or how hard it gets, I'm going to make it."

- Les Brown

152- If it is bringing you down and causing you pain, LET IT GO. You don't need negativity in your life.

- Susan Flynn

153- Talk sense to a fool, and he calls you foolish.

- Euripides

154- How natural it is to destroy what we cannot possess, to deny what we do not understand, and to insult what we envy.

- Honoré de Balzac

155- We should remember that nothing lasts forever. Time is precious and should not be wasted on hatred, envy, greed, or self-pity. We must enjoy life and always remind ourseleves how blessed we are.

- Susan Flynn

156- It is easy to sit back and take notice; what is difficult is getting up and taking action.

- Honoré de Balzac

157- Real power is not revealed by striking hard or often but by striking true. The hardest thing in life is to make a choice.

- Honoré de Balzac

158- True love is eternal, infinite, and always itself. It is equal and pure. Hatred is the vice of narrow souls; they feed it with all their littleness and make it the pretext of base tyrannies.

- Honoré de Balzac

159- Life isn't fair, but it's still good. When in doubt, just take the next small step.
Life is too short to waste time hating anyone.
Don't take yourself so seriously; no one else does.
Pay off your credit cards every month.
You don't have to win every argument.

Agree to disagree sometimes.

Cry with someone; it's more healing than crying alone.

Save for retirement, starting with your first payslip.

- Regina Brett, spiritual speaker

160- We don't realize our strength until we are faced with our greatest weakness or fear.

- Susan Flynn

161- People who are crazy enough to think they can change the world are the ones who do it.

- Rob Siltanen

162- Develop an attitude of gratitude; say thank you to everyone you meet for everything they do for you.

- Brian Tracy

163- Live your life so that the fear of death can never enter your heart. Trouble no one for their religion; respect others on their view and demand that they respect you too.

- Chief Tecumseh

164- Love your life; perfect your life; beautify all things in your life. Seek to make your life long and its purpose in the service of your people. Prepare a noble death song for the day when you pass over the great divide.

- Chief Tecumseh

165- I can't give a sure-fire formula for success, but I can give you a formula for failure. Try to please everybody all the time.

- Herbert Swope

166- Do what you feel in your heart is right for you will be criticized anyway.

- Eleanor Roosevelt

167- When I despair, I remember that all through history, the way of truth and love has always won. There have been tyrants and murderers, and for the time, they can seem invincible, but in the end, they always fall; think of it, always.

- Gandhi

168- Life isn't about finding yourself; life is about creating yourself.

- George Bernard

169- Do what you can with what you have where you are.

- Theodore Roosevelt

170- When you show yourself to the world and display your talents, you naturally stir up all kinds of resentments, envy, and other manifestations of insecurity. You cannot spend your life worrying about the petty feelings of others.

- Robert Greene

171- The difference between a successful person and others is not a lack of strength, not a lack of knowledge, but rather, a lack in will.

- Vince Lombardi

172- Imperfection is beauty, madness is genius, and it's better to be absolutely ridiculous than absolutely boring.

- Marilyn Monroe

173- I have not failed; I have just found 10,000 ways that won't work.

- Thomas Edison

174- There are only two ways to live your life: one is as though nothing is a miracle; the other is as though everything is a miracle.
- Albert Einstein

175- Fairy tales are more than true, not because they tell us that dragons exist but because they tell us that dragons can be beaten.
- Neil Gaiman

176- Yesterday is history; tomorrow is a mystery. Today is the gift of God, which is why we call it the present.
- Bil Keane

177- I'm enough of an artist to draw freely upon my imagination. Imagination is more important than knowledge. Knowledge is limited. Imagination encircles the world.
- Albert Einstein

178- Success is not final; failure is not fatal. It's the courage to continue that counts.
- Winston Churchill

179- Success is getting what you want, happiness is wanting what you get.
- Dale Carnegie

180- Just be yourself because everyone else is already taken. The way to get started is to quit talking and begin doing.
- Oscar Wilde

181- Winners are not afraid of losing, but losers are. Failure is a part of the process of success. People who avoid failure also avoid success.

- Robert Kiyosaki

182- I have learned that success is to be measured not so much by the position that one has reached in life as by the obstacles which he has overcome while trying to succeed.

- Booker T. Washington

183- I've come to believe that each of us has a personal calling that is unique as a fingerprint and that the best way to succeed is to discover what you love and then find a way to offer it to others in the form of service, working hard and also allowing the energy of the universe to lead you.

- Oprah Winfrey

184- Success does not consist in never making mistakes but in never making the same one a second time.

- George Bernard

185- To each, there comes in their lifetime a special moment when they are figuratively tapped on the shoulder and offered the chance to do a very special thing, unique to them and fitted to their talents; what a tragedy if that moment finds them unprepared or unqualified for that which could have been their finest hour.

- Winston Churchill

186- He is not perfect, you aren't either, and the two of you will never be perfect, but if he can make you laugh at least once, causes you to think twice, and if he admits to being human and making mistakes, hold onto him and give him the most you can.

- Bob Marley

187- When you get to the point where you candidly don't care what anyone else thinks of you, you have reached a dangerously awesome level of freedom.

- Susan Flynn

188- You act like a mortal in all that you fear and like immortal in all that you desire.

- Lucius A Seneca

189- All you need in this life is ignorance and confidence; then success is sure.

- Mark Twain

190- You've gotta dance like there's nobody watching, love like you'll never be hurt, sing like there's nobody listening, and live like it's heaven on earth.

- William Purkey

191- Do not train a child to learn by force or harshness, but direct them to it by what amuses their mind so that you may be better able to discover with accuracy the peculiar bent of the genius of each.

- Plato

192- And I said to my body, softly,
"I want to be your friend." It took a long breath and replied, "I have been waiting my whole life for this."

- Nayyirah Waheed

193- There are three classes of men: lovers of wisdom, lovers of honor, and lovers of gain.

- Plato

194- Courage is knowing what not to fear. There is no easy way from the earth to the stars. Most powerful is he who has himself in his own power.
Difficulties strengthen the mind as labor does the body.

- Seneca

195- I am the wisest man alive for I know one thing, and that is that I know nothing.

- Plato

196- As long as you live, you should keep learning how to live.

- Seneca

197- Good people do not need laws to tell them how to act responsibly, while bad people will find a way around the laws.

- Plato

198- Don't judge each day by the harvest you reap but the seed you plant.

- Robert L. Stevenson

199- Clear your heart and mind of all "people guilt;" stop carrying around the responsibility for how everyone feels toward you. We don't have to be the "host" at everyone's pity party.

- Susan Flynn

200- Toxic people project their own character defects onto their victim. They do this by accusing the victim of the exact action they themselves do but deny.

- Shannon Thomas

201- Don't worry about the mistakes; worry about the chances you miss when you never try.

- Jack Canfield

202- If your dreams don't scare you, they aren't big enough. Education costs money. But then, so does ignorance.

- Sir Claus Moser

203- Nobody ever wrote down a plan to be broken, fat, lazy, or stupid. Those things are what happen when you don't have a plan.

- Larry Winget

204-There is no need to cut negetave people out of your life. Just keep working on yourself, and as you grow, they will fall off.

- Susan Flynn

205- Self-confidence is a superpower. Once you start believing in yourself, magic starts happening.

- Lauryn Hoover

206- Complaining will attract things to complain about; gratitude will attract things to be grateful about.

- Susan Flynn

207- Remember, most of your stress comes from the way you respond, not the way life is. Adjust your attitude, and all that extra stress is gone.

- Idil Ahmed

208- Be willing to walk alone; many who have started with you won't finish with you. Every experience, no matter how bad it seems, holds within it a blessing of the same kind. The gold is to find it.

- Buddha

209- Why not be the reason someone's not hungry today? Why does someone smile today, feel loved, and believes in the goodness in people.

- Susan Flynn

210- Keep away from people who try to belittle your ambitions. Small people always do that, but the great make you feel that you too can become great.

- Mark Twain

211- Never allow someone to be your priority while allowing yourself to be their option.

- Mark Twain

212- Kindness is the language that the deaf can hear and the blind can see.

- Mark Twain

213- The most difficult thing is the decision to act. The rest is merely tenacity; the fears are paper tigers. You can do anything you decide to do. You can act to change and control your life and the procedure, the process, and its rewards.

- Amelia Earhart

214- I will not follow where the path may lead, but I will go where there is no path, and I will leave a trail.

- Muriel Strode

215- Whatever you can do or dream, you can begin it. Boldness has genius, power, and magic in it.

- Johann Wolfgang

216- If you want happiness for an hour, take a nap. If you want happiness for a day, go fishing. If you want happiness for a year, inherit a fortune. If you want happiness for a lifetime, help someone else.

- Chinese Proverb

217- Twenty years from now, you will be more disappointed by the things you didn't do than by the one you did do, so throw off the bowlines; sail away from the safe harbor. Catch the trade wind in your sail. Explore, dream, discover.

- Mark Twain

218- I have learned over the years that when one's mind is made up, this diminishes fears.

- Rosa Park

219- You don't need a better phone; you don't need a better home; you don't need better circumstances. You need a better mindset.

- Matthew Toren

220- I slept, and I dreamed that life is all joy. I woke up, and I saw that life is all service. I served and saw that service is joy.

-Reinhold Niebuhr

221- Time is too slow for those who wait, too swift for those who fear, too long for those who grieve, too short for those who rejoice, but for those who love, time is eternity.

- Henry Van Dyke

222- When I started counting my blessings, my whole life turned around.

- Willie Nelson

223- Kindness doesn't cost anything; therefore, we should be kind to everyone we meet because everyone is fighting a battle of some kind. We walk around with a smile even though we're broken.

- Susan Flynn

224- Challenges are what make life interesting, and overcoming them is what makes life meaningful.

- Josh J Marine

225- Wise men speak because they have something to say. We become just by doing just acts, temperate by doing temperate acts, brave by doing brave acts.

- Aristotle

226- I will never again settle for a mediocre, average existence. I will think big and ask big. Then I will experience BIG. I deserve all the great things this life has to offer, I am NOT an excuse maker. I am always improving my life and the lives of everyone around me.

- Susan Flynn

227- The energy of the mind is the essence of life.

- Aristotle

228- The will to win, the desire to succeed, the urge to reach your full potential—these are the keys that will unlock the door to personal excellence.

- Confucius

229- Do the difficult things while they are easy and do the great things while they are small. A journey of a thousand miles must begin with a single step.

- Lao Tzu

230- Always start your day with positive energy. Speak and think positively; think healing, think happiness, think big.

- Susan Flynn

231- Good character is not formed in a week or a month. It is created little by little. Day by day, protracted and patient, the effort is needed to develop the character.

- Hercules

232- Life's most persistent and urgent question is, WHAT ARE WE DOING FOR OTHERS?

- Dr. Martin Luther King

233- Happy is the man who has broken the chains which hurt the mind and has given up worrying once and for all.

- Ovid

234- The superior man is distressed by the limitations of his abilities. He is not distressed by the fact that men do not recognize the ability that he has.

- Confucius

235-LUCK is what happens when preparation meets opportunities.

- Seneca

236- If you ever had to encounter even one of these in your life-time, a hungry stomach, an empty pocket, and a broken heart, you will learn the most valuable lessons in life.

- Susan Flynn

237- Don't break a bird's wing and then tell it to fly. Don't break a heart and then tell it to love. Don't break a soul and then tell it to be happy. Don't see the worst in a person and expect them to see the best in you. Don't judge and expect them to stand by your side. Don't play with fire and expect to stay perfectly safe. You cannot expect to give bad and receive good.

- Najwa Zabian

238- If you fall in love with life and just be a happy, grateful, accepting, caring, warm, kind human being, together you will help change the world.

- Susan Flynn

239- No one has the right to judge because no one really knows what you have been through. Everyone has been or is going through something in their life, and they didn't feel what you felt in your heart, let us be kind to one another.

- Susan Flynn

240- Some of our best days are still ahead of us. Just be yourself and let the world see the real Imperfect, Flawed, Quirky, Beautiful, and Magical person that you are.

- Susan Flynn

241- When I'm asked, "How do you still stand strong after all you've been through?" I say, "I am a SURVIVOR, not a victim."

- Susan Flynn

242- Your body is just a scoop of earth. Carry it gracefully, and when it's time to put it back, put it back gracefully.

- Sadhguru

243- If you believe you can benefit by causing suffering to someone else, it will not only be a temporary benefit— you will also pay for it in ways that you will not understand or be able to bear. No one can escape this. Karma is not a concept of crime and punishment that if you commit a crime, someone punishes you. Karma is a consequence of your action. If you throw a stone up, gravity is not trying to hit you with a stone. It's your stone which comes back and knocks you on your head THAT IS KARMA.

- Mahabharat

244- How profound is your experience of life, and how impactful are you in what you do? This is all that really matters in life.

- Sadhguru

245- If money and material things
make you believe that you are better than others, you are the poorest person on earth because love, kindness, compassion, and loyalty are some of the things money can't buy.

- Susan Flynn

246- Passion is focused on one thing; therefore, it burns out at some point. Compassion is all-inclusive. It has so much fuel to burn that it does not die out.

- Sadhguru

247- Remember, the life in front of you is more important than the life behind you. Don't live in your past. It was just a lesson, not a life sentence.

- Susan Flynn

248- Being able to have stimulating conversations with the right person is priceless.

- Susan Flynn

249- What do you need to do when you are triggered by a person or a situation? When you are triggered, go within and feel. Don't act or react; don't explain or try to prove that you are right. This is the ego trying to control everything and always waiting to have the last word. It doesn't matter what is true, what is right or wrong, whose opinion counts, and who we should listen to. We all have our own truth, and it doesn't have to be the same as everyone else. Find your truth. When you are triggered, this means that there is something you need to see, feel, understand, observe, and experience to move forward. Listen to the silence of your soul, and you will figure things out. Ask yourself, "What do I need to see? What do I need to feel? What do I need to know? How can I nurture myself and love myself? What does my inner child crave? What is my inner child showing?" Your heart knows the way.

- Unknown

250- On this journey called life, you will realize there is a purpose for everyone you meet. Some will love you, some will use you, some will try to break you, but everyone will teach you. The ones who are truly important are the ones that stand by you and bring out the best in you. They are the amazing people who remind you why you must not give up.

- Susan Flynn

251- Strong people not only feel pain; they accept it, learn from it, and fight through it. They turn their pain into strength, they take a break, dust themselves off, get back up and fight as they have never fought before.

- Susan Flynn

252- KINDNESS:
One of the greatest gifts you can bestow upon another. If someone is in need, lend them a helping hand. Do not wait for a thank you. True kindness lies within the act of giving without the expectation of something in return.

- Katharine Hepburn

253- Learn how to lead your heart. Start recognizing when something isn't good for you and be strong enough to let it go. A person can only waste the time you allow them to waste. Stop trying to open doors to people who constantly shut you out. Make sure the trust is shown in the effort, the talk is supported by the action, and the trust is earned through consistency.

- Rob Hill Sr.

254- A lot of walking away will do your life good. Walk away from arguments that lead you to anger and nowhere. Walk away from people who deliberately put you down. Walk away from the practice of pleasing people who choose to never see your worth. Walk away from any thought that undermines your peace of mind. Walk away from judgmental people; they do not know the struggle you are facing and what you have been through. Walk away from your mistakes and fears; they do not determine your fate. The more you walk away from things that poison your soul, the healthier your life will be.

- Dodinsky

255- Learn to control your thoughts, and you will learn to control your behavior because your thoughts becomes your words and your actions.

- Susan Flynn

256- I have endured pain and struggles. I have felt loss. I have been broken. I have known hardship. I have stood alone. But here I am, moving forward, one day at a time. I will remember the lessons I have learned in my life because they are the reason I am still standing stronger than before.

- Susan Flynn

257- Stay true to yourself. Don't worry about what people think of you or about the way they try to make you feel. If people want to see you as a good person, they will. If they want to see you as a bad person, absolutely nothing you do will stop them. Ironically, the more you try to show them your good intentions, the more you give them to knock you down. If they are committed to misunderstanding you, keep your head up high and be confident in your intentions and keep your eyes ahead instead of wasting your time on those who want to drag you back. Because you can't change people's views, you have to believe that true change for yourself comes from within you, not from anyone else.

- Najwa Zebian

258- Speak positive words into your life every single morning. Think big, think healing, think success, think peace, think happiness, think growth mindset, and always start the day with positive energy—you deserve it.

- Sylvester McNutt

259-Whenever you do not understand what is happening in your life, just close your eyes, take a deep breath, and say, "God, I know it's Your plan; just help me through it."

- Alberto Casing

260- Happiness is a choice, not a result. Nothing will make you happy until you choose to be happy. No person will make you happy unless you decide to be happy. Your happiness will not come to you; it can only come from you.

- Ralph Marston

261- The fact of the matter is, we don't know what tomorrow will bring. The only thing we have is right now. So, don't stay mad for too long. Learn to forgive and love with all your heart. Live every day. Don't worry about who doesn't like you. Love the ones who do.

- Susan Flynn

262- We have a choice each and every day of our life. I choose to feel blessed, be grateful, feel excited, be thankful, be happy, and think positively.

- Susan Flynn

263- You never really know the true impact you have on those around you. You never know how much someone needed that smile you gave them. You never know how much your kindness turned someone's entire life around. You never know how much someone needed that long hug or deep talk. So, don't wait to be kind. Don't wait for better circumstances or for someone to change. Just be kind because you never know how much someone needs it.

- Nikki Banas

264- It is important to take a break from everything and concentrate on yourself. You are not responsible for fixing everything and everyone that is broken. You don't always have to make everyone else happy. Be sure to make your own happiness and peace of mind a priority.

- Susan Flynn

265- When nobody else celebrates you, learn to celebrate yourself. When nobody else compliments you, then compliment yourself. It's not up to other people to keep you encouraged; it's up to you. Encouragement should come from the inside.

- Joel Osteen

266- We maintain peace through our strength; weakness only invites aggression.

-Ronald Reagan

267- Five things you will never recover in life:
A stone after it's thrown
A word after it's said
An occasion after it's missed
Time after it's gone
Trust after it's lost.

- Janice Conklin

268- Speak in such a way that others love to listen to you. Listen in such a way that others love to speak to you.

-Zig Ziglar

269- I choose to live by choice, not by chance. To be motivated, not manipulated. To be useful, not used. To make changes, not excuses. To excel, not compete. I choose self-esteem, not self–pity. I choose to listen to my inner voice, not to the random opinions of others.

- Marranda Marrott

270- Be good to everyone without expectation. If someone disrespects you, walk away. Don't seek revenge or put yourself in a position that ruins your soul. Keep peace in your heart always.

- Susan Flynn

271- If you let a person talk long enough, you'll hear their true intentions. Listen twice, speak once.

- Tupac Shakur

272- If you hate a person, then you are defeated by that person. Your peace is more important than driving yourself crazy trying to understand why something happened the way it did; let it go.

- Mandy Hale

273 -You are not weak, you are not small, you are not a disappointment. You are everything that you are supposed to be for a reason, and one day, you will realize that all those broken pieces were stepping stones to create a better you.

- Roger Lee

274- Don't take things personally. It isn't always about you. Don't become the victim in someone else's drama.

- Susan Flynn

275- Hey you, you're holding onto too many bags. You can't do it all, you can't be it all, you can't carry it all. Do what you can, be who you are, only carry what's IMPORTANT, and put the rest of the bags down.

- Amy Weatherly

276- Never give up, never lose hope, always have faith. It allows you to cope. Trying times will pass, as they always do. Just have patience; your dreams will come true. So, put on your smile; you will live through your pain. Know it will pass and strength will gain.

- Charlie Remiggio

277- Self-control is strength. When you get to a point where your mood doesn't shift based upon someone else's actions or words, it is called intelligence.

- Susan Flynn

278- Reflect upon your present blessing of which every man has plenty, not on your past misfortunes of which all men have some.

- Charles Dickens

279 Reminder: you can always start over, get a fresh start, make a change, be afraid, be careful, be uncertain, fail again and again, and still succeed.

- Susan Flynn

280- Gossips are worse than thieves because they steal another person's dignity, honest reputation, and credibility, which are challenging to restore. Remember, when your feet slip, you can always recover your balance, but when your tongue slips, you cannot recover your words.

- Karen Salmansohn

281- How far you go in life depends on your tenderness with the young, compassionate with the aged, sympathetic with the striving, and tolerance of the weak and the strong because someday in life, you will have been all of these.

- George Washington

282- Never become too attached to anyone because attachment leads to expectations, and expectations lead to disappointment, pain and suffering.

- Susan Flynn

283- You must leave your past in the past because if you don't, it will destroy your future. Enjoy what today has to offer, and forget what yesterday has taken from you.

- Susan Flynn

284- There is only one way to happiness, and that is to cease worrying about things that are beyond the power of our will.

- Epictetus

285- Your mind is a garden; your thoughts are the seeds. You can grow flowers, or you can grow weeds.

- Sunflower Gardener

286- When tensions rise like the ocean tides and you can see no shore in sight, just call on me, and I'll be there to see you through the night.

- Jimmy Osborne

287- No one is perfect. We all make mistakes. We say the wrong things. We do wrong things. We learn, we grow, we move on, we live, and we should be grateful every day for being blessed with another chance.

- Susan Flynn

288- Learn to be open-minded and respectful to other people's religion, culture, and opinions, even if you don't agree.

- Susan Flynn

289- *I am strong because I know my weakness.

*I am compassionate because I've suffered.

*I am alive because I am a fighter.

*I am wise because I've been foolish.

*I can laugh because I have known sadness.

*I can love because I've known loss.

*I am a strong woman who has weathered the storm but still loves to dance in the rain.

- Ziad K. Abdelnour

290- With everything that has happened to you, you can either feel sorry for yourself or treat what happened as a gift. Everything is either an opportunity to grow or an obstacle to keep you from growing (you get to choose).

- Wayne Dyer

291- Within you lies the STRENGTH to rise above any situation you might be facing. That strength will transform you into the most beautiful version of yourself.

- Susan Flynn

292- I no longer allow people to disturb my peace. I deserve peace, and I am allowed to choose who I want in my life. This life is the only thing that is truly mine, and I refuse to feel guilty for wanting serenity.

- Susan Flynn

293- Allowing people inside your life is a beautiful thing; letting people go who drain your spirit is another beautiful thing you can do for your life. The key to being happy is knowing you have the power to choose what to accept and what to let go.

- Dodinsky

294- Death is not the greatest loss in life; the greatest loss is what dies inside us while we live.

- Buddha

295- Saying goodbye to someone we love is the hardest thing, but sometimes they are the ones who are slowly killing us inside.

-Susan Flynn

296- I recognize my brilliance, and I allow my mind to rest. I recognize my worth, and I allow my soul to rest. I am able to accept abundance into my life.

-Susan Flynn

297- I have the utmost respect for anyone who can put their ego aside and say, "I made a mistake. I apologize, and I am going to correct my behavior."

-Susan Flynn

298- You cannot control how other people receive your energy. Anything you do and say gets filtered through the lens of whatever personal stuff they are going through at the moment, which is not about you. Just keep doing you with integrity, love, and understanding.

-Nancy Hoffman

299- On this journey, you should take the good with the bad. Always forgive, but never forget. Learn from your mistakes. People change. Just remember, life goes on.

-Susan Flynn

300- When you finally learn a person's behavior has more to do with their internal struggle than it ever did with you, YOU LEARN GRACE.

-Allison Aars

301- If you love someone, cherish them. Most importantly, show them. Life is very fragile. Don't take anyone for granted. Say what you need to say, love hard, then love some more. Love too much. Remember, everything is temporary, but love outlives us all.

- Susan Flynn

302-Use pain as a stepping stone, not as a camping ground.

- Alan Cohen

303- Life is for living. Open the windows. Turn up the music loud. Let your hair down and DANCE! Check in on the people you love. Go for a long walk. Enjoy the beautiful show nature is putting on for us, and feel alive.

- Susan Flynn

304- One day, you are going to wake up and realize how strong you were, how brave you were, and how beautiful every single day of your life really is.

-Susan Flynn

305- Faith is not pretending that troubles don't exist. Faith is knowing it won't last forever, pain and hurt will heal, difficulties will overcome, and we will be led out of the darkness.

-Susan Flynn

306- The biggest lesson I've learned is: it is okay. It's okay for me to be kind to myself. It's okay to be wrong. It's okay to get mad. It's okay to be flawed. It's okay to be happy. It's ok to move on.

-Hailey Williams

307- Open yourself to the world and allow for it to fill that space with the kinds of people, the kinds of moments, and the kinds of experiences that exhilarate you, that compel you, that make you love yourself and your life and what you have to offer more and more each day.

-Bianca Sparacino

308- Sometimes courage is a quiet fight, a dim softness within you that flickers even on your darkest day and reminds you that you are strong, that you are growing, that there is hope.

-Bianca Sparacino

309- LOVELY THING TO LEARN. Adjust yourself in every situation and any shape. But most importantly, find your way to flow.

-Buddha

310- Always be calm but alert, relaxed but ready, smooth but sharp, be humble but confident. And most of all, always be loving and kind.

-Susan Flynn

311- One day, we'll forget our pain, our tears, and the reason we cried. We will realize the secret of being free is not revenge but letting things unfold in their own way and time.

-Susan Flynn

312- To make a difference in someone's life, you don't have to be brilliant, rich, beautiful, perfect. You just have to care.

- Mandy Hale

313- Some people could be given an entire field of roses and only see the thorns in it. Others could be given a single weed and only see the wildflower in it. Perfection is a key component of gratitude, and gratitude is a key component to joy.

- Amy Weatherly

314- You should create a world of beauty with your attitude, your behavior, and your actions.

- Susan Flynn

315- Don't connect with toxic people just because you're lonely; you don't drink poison just because you are thirsty.

-Susan Flynn

316- Worry about your character, not your reputation. Your character is who you are; your reputation is who people think you are.

-John Wooden

317- One of the biggest signs of maturity is being able to disagree with someone while still being respectful.

-Dave Willis

318- Be the one who nurtures and builds. Be the one who has an understanding and a forgiving heart, one who looks for the best in people. Leave people better than you found them.

-Marvin J. Ashton

319- Every day is a gift, a new beginning, a chance for a do-over. So, take a deep breath, smile, say THANK YOU, THANK YOU, THANK YOU and begin again.

- Susan Flynn

320- I am a woman's woman. I won't run off with your man. I won't hate you because you are beautiful. I will celebrate your success. I'll listen to you when you're in pain. I will stand by you. I choose my friends carefully, and if I choose you, I will love you with all my heart.

- Susan Flynn

321- Most of us say, "I am sorry," after making a mistake. Only a few ask, "What can I do to make it right?"

- Susan Flynn

322- Living life to the fullest? It's waking up every morning with no regrets. It's knowing you deserve to be happy and be loved. It's doing what's right in your heart. It's about being yourself because no one can tell you you're doing wrong.

- Susan Flynn

323- If you pay attention to the patterns in your life, you will realize everything always works out for the best in the end. because you are always evolving, and the things you think you can't survive, somehow you divinely make it through.

- Susan Flynn

324- When death comes for me, dress me elegantly with a crown made of leaves from green elephant trees. O, plant me a seed sown so delicately that it grows up to be an umbrella for thee. And when you are grieved, come sit under my leaves. Let them speak memories on the eloquent breeze. Leave me your sorrow. Sing me sweet elegies. Let me borrow your fear by the birds' melodies. So, swallow your tears; please don't mourn much for me for I'll always be here in the form of a tree.

-Jimmy Osborne

325- If you are holding onto anger against someone who hurt you in the past, they are still hurting you today. The injury still bleeds.

Forgiveness is not for the people who hurt you; forgiveness is for you so you can move on.

- Susan Flynn

326- Use your voice to speak of wisdom, your hands for charity, your words for truth, and your heart for compassion and LOVE.

- Susan Flynn

327- Life is always changing. You lose loved ones. You lose a piece of yourself you never imagined would be gone, and then without even realizing it, new love enters your life and new friends come along. Then one day, there is going to be a stronger, wiser, you staring back in the mirror.

- Susan Flynn

328- You cannot change all the people around you, However you can change the people you choose to be around.

- Susan Flynn

329- I live my life like a river–I never go in reverse; what is done is done. I forget the past. I look ahead and always stay positive.

- Susan Flynn

330- If you fail, never give up because F.A.I.L. means "first attempt in learning." It is not the end; in fact, E.N.D. means "effort never dies." If you get no as an answer, remember N.O. means "next opportunity," so let's be positive."

- Dr. Abdul Kalam

INDEX

1. Unknown–Goodread.com

2. Unknown–this is an old Indian song translated into English.

3. Tony McCollum–Goodreads.com

4. Susan Flynn

5. Susan Flynn

6. Susan Flynn

7. Ellen DeGeneres: one of America's most famous talk show host–Brainyquotes.com

8. Kahlil Gibran. He was a Lebanese American writer and poet–Forbesquotes.com

9. Jim Rohn was an American author and motivational speaker.

10. Susan Flynn

11. Susan Flynn

12. John Maxwell–an American author, speaker, and pastor.

13. Susan Flynn

14. Bhagavad Gita–Indian holy book

15. Susan Flynn

16. Susan Flynn

17. Buddha–a spiritual teacher from the Indian subcontinent.

18. Susan Flynn

19. Ralph Waldo Emerson–philosopher, lecturer, and poet.

20. Bhagavad Gita–Indian holy book.

21. Rumi–Turkish scholar and most famous for his well-known poems.

22. Brandon Bay–motivational speaker and best-selling author.

23. Susan Flynn

24. Thomas Carlyle–English historian, www.brainy quotes.com.

25. Unknown–www.green villeisd.com

26. Susan Flynn

27. Mahatma Gandhi–an Indian lawyer, civil rights movement activist. Lived from 1869-1968.

28. Charlie Chaplin–an English comic actor who lived from 1889-1977.

29. Marilyn Monroe–an American actress and model. Lived from 1926-1962.

30. James Allen–British author, brainyquotes.com

31. Susan Flynn

32. Buddha–Tinybuddha.com

33. Susan Colton–an American author.

34. Mahatma Gandhi–nationalist and political ethicist.

35. Jay Shetty–a former monk and bestselling author.

36. Susan Flynn

37. Mahatma Gandhi–anti colonial, nationalist, and political ethicist.

38. Walt Whitman– American poet.

39. Mother Teresa–Indian saint missionary.

40. Soren Kierkegaard– Danish poet who lived from 1813-1855.

41. Mahatma Gandhi

42. Mahatma Gandhi, civil rights movement.

43. Chief Yellow Lark

44. Susan Flynn

45. Susan Flynn

46. Kelly's Treehouse–www.pinterest.kellytreehouse.com

47. Saint Francis–Italian Catholic friar.

48. Will Smith–American actor.

49. Rebecca Fox–American actress, www.pinterest.com.

50. Susan Flynn

51. Susan Flynn

52. Susan Flynn

53. Souza–www.scrapbook.com.

54. Jay Shetty–Former Hindu monk, author, and life coach of Indian descent.

55. Susan Flynn

56. Marcus Aurelius– former Roman emperor- lived AD 121-AD 180.

57. Susan Flynn

58. Albert Szent–Hungarian Nobel Prize winner.

59. Susan Flynn

60. Susan Flynn

61. Unknown–www.pinterest.com

62. Deepak Chopra–Indian-born American author.

63. Michael Jordan–one of the greatest basketball players of all time.

64. Susan Flynn

65. Bruce Lee–martial arts instructor and actor, lived 1940-1973.

66. Ken Keyes, Jr.–an American author and lecturer.

67. Susan Flynn

68. Anne Frank–victim of the Holocaust and a German-Dutch diarist of Jewish heritage.

69. Susan Flynn

70. Deepak Chopra–author and alternative medicine advocate.

71. Sir Richard Branson–author, www.goodreads.com.

72. Susan Flynn

73. Susan Flynn

74. Susan Flynn

75. Susan Flynn

76. Susan Flynn

77. Susan Flynn

78. Zig Ziglar–an American author and motivational speaker.

79. Buddha

80. Susan Flynn

81. Paulo Coelho–Brazilian lyricist and novelist, blog.moving-worlds.org.

82. Susan Flynn

83. Susan Flynn

84. Susan Flynn

85. Unknown–goodreads.com

86. Lester Levenson– successful entrepreneur.

87. Susan Flynn

88. Flavia Weedn–an author on spirituality and love.

89. C.S. Lewis–a British writer.

90. John Trudell–Native American author.

91. Susan Flynn

92. Susan Flynn

93. Susan Flynn

94. Zig Ziglar–was an American author and motivational speaker.

95. William D Hoard–a politician and newspaper editor.

96. Bryon Katie–an American author and speaker.

97. Susan Flynn

98. Susan Flynn

99. Ajahn Chah–Buddhist monk and lived from 1918-1992.

100. Roger Lee–Chinese American architect, www.wikipedia.org.

101. Susan Flynn

102. Lisa Villa Prosen– author, coach, and speaker, www.pinterest.com.

103. Susan Flynn

104. Susan Flynn

105. Susan Flynn

106. Susan Flynn

107. Susan Flynn

108. Sadhguru

109. Rehman Khan–author and doctor.

110. Bhagavad Gita– Hindu holy book.

111. Mother Teresa–Catholic saint of Calcutta, India.

112. Mother Teresa–nun and missionary.

113. Mother Teresa

114. Buddha–tinybuddha.com.

115. Mother Teresa

116. Mother Teresa–Nobel Peace Prize winner.

117. John F Kennedy–35th American president.

118. Mother Teresa

119. Mother Teresa

120. Amanda Rose–American author.

121. Bhagavad Gita–Hindu holy book

122. Bhagavad Gita

123. Buddha quotes–tinybuddha.com.

124. Susan Flynn

125. Dolly Parton–one of America's most-loved country singer icons.

126. Richard L. Eve–American author, brainyquote.com.

127. Rebekka Redd–accomplished global fly angler and published writer.

128. Buddha–tinybuddha.com.

129. Stuart Scott–an American sports actor of the football league.

130. Albert Camus–French philosopher and author.

131. Henry James–British author born in America, wikipedia.org.

132. Mark Twain American writer, publisher; he was lauded as the greatest humorist the United States has produced.

133. Ziad. K. Abdelnour–author and banking advocate, wikipedia.org.

134. Bhagavad Gita

135. Susan Flynn

136. Susan Flynn

137. Mark Twain–writer and publisher.

138. Doug Larson–editor and columnist, wikipedia.org.

139. Mark Twain–American humorist.

140. Charles Dickens–English writer.

141. Charles Dickens–English writer and social critic.

142. Euripides–Greek wisdom, classicalwisdom.com.

143. Kalyani Lawry–teacher and an inspirational speaker.

144. Buddha–tinybuddha.com.

145. Dalai Lama– spiritual leader, travelandleisure.com.

146. Euripides–Greek wisdom, www.classicalwisdom.com.

147. Susan Flynn

148. Euripides–tragedy of classical Athens.

149. Euripides

150. Euripides–one of the three ancient Greek tragedians.

151. Les Brown–politician and motivational speaker.

152. Susan Flynn

153. Euripides

154. Honoré de Balzac–French novelist and playwright.

155. Susan Flynn

156. Honoré de Balzac–French writer, wikipedia.org.

157. Honoré de Balzac

158. Honoré de Balzac

159. Regina Brett–American author and inspirational speaker.

160. Susan Flynn

161. Rob Siltanen–a leading creative marketer www. linkedin.com.

162. Brian Tracy–Canadian-American public speaker.

163. Chief Tecumseh–Shawnee chief and warrior.

164. Chief Tecumseh–formed a Native American confederacy and promoted unity.

165. Herbert Swope–American journalist and editor.

166. Eleanor Roosevelt–American political figure and activist.

167. Mahatma Gandhi

168. George Benard Shaw–Irish playwright and political activist.

169. Theodore Roosevelt– United States 26th president.

170. Robert Greene–American author on seduction and power.

171. Vince Lombardi–National Football League football coach.

172. Marilyn Monroe– American actress and model.

173. Thomas Edison investor and businessman. He developed devices such as mass communication and sound recording.

174. Albert Einstein–one of the most influential physicists of all time.

175. Neil Gaiman–English writer of novels, comics, and films.

176. Bil Keane–American cartoonist most notable for newspaper comic "Family Circus."

177. Albert Einstein– German-born theoretical physicist.

178. Winston Churchill

179. Dale Carnegie–American writer and lecturer.

180. Oscar Wilde–Irish playwright and poet.

181. Robert Kiyosaki– author, www.goodreads.com.

182. Booker T. Washington–dominant leader in the African American community.

183. Oprah Winfrey– American talk show host, actress, and author.

184. George Bernard–was an Irish play writer, polemicist, and political activist.

185. Winston Churchill– British prime minister of the United Kingdom from 1940 to 1945 and again from 1951 to 1955.

186. Bob Marley–Jamaican singer and songwriter.

187. Susan Flynn

188. Lucius A Seneca–Roman Stoic, philosopher, and statesman.

189. Mark Twain

190. William Purkey–professor emeritus of counselor education, crowin.com.

191. Plato–philosopher during the 5th century BCE.

192. Nayyirah Waheed–poet and author, wikipedia.org.

193. Plato

194. Seneca–Roman Stoic.

195. Plato–was a philosopher.

196. Seneca

197. Plato

198. Robert L Stevenson

199. Susan Flynn

200. Shannon Thomas–best-selling author exposing financial abuse.

201. Jack Canfield–American author and motivational speaker.

202. Sir Claus Moser–was a British statistician.

203. Larry Winget–social commentator, author, and professional speaker.

204. Susan Flynn

205. Lauryn Hoover–actress and producer, instagram.com.

206. Susan Flynn

207. Idil Ahmed–author and social media influencer, instagram.com.

208. Buddha–tinybuddha.com.

209. Susan Flynn

210. Mark Twain: his real name was Samuel Langhorn Clemens. He was an American author and humorist.

211. Mark Twain–mark twain house.org.

212. Mark Twain– mark twain house.org.

213. Amelia Earhart–was an American aviation pioneer and author.

214. Muriel Strode–was an American poet. She was a member of the Poetry Society of America.

215. Johann Wolfgang–was a German poet, playwright, and novelist, brainyquotes.com.

216- Chinese Proverb– thoughtco.com.

217. Mark Twain– mark twain house.org.

218. Rosa Parks–was an American activist in the Civil Rights Movement.

219. Matthew Toren–mentor, and co-founder of young entrepreneurs.

220. Reinhold Nibuhr–American Protestant theologian.

221. Henry Vandyke–was an American author, educator, and diplomat.

222. Willie Nelson–American musician, actor and activist, willienelson.com.

223. Susan Flynn

224. Josh J Marine–an author and known for his famous quotes.

225. Aristotle–was a Greek philosopher.

226. Susan Flynn

227. Aristotle–www.goodreads.com.

228. Confucius–was a Chinese philosopher and politician.

229. Lao Tzu–was an ancient Chinese writer, www.goodreads.com.

230. Susan Flynn

231. Hercules–is the Roman equivalent of the Greek divine hero.

232. Martin Luther King–was an American leader and spokesman in the Civil Rights Movement.

233. Ovid–was the first major Roman poet, goodreads.com.

234. Confucius–thoughtco.com.

235. Seneca Lucius Annaeus–Seneca was a roman Stoic, graco usquotes.com.

236. Susan Flynn

237. Najwa Zabian–is a Lebanese-Canadian activist, poet, and speaker, goodreads.com.

238. Susan Flynn

239. Susan Flynn

240. Susan Flynn

241. Susan Flynn

242. Sadhguru Jagadish Jaggi Vasudav–is an Indian yoga guru, sadhguru.org.

243. Mahabharat–is one of the two major Sanskrit epics of ancient India.

244. Sadhguru–sadhguru.org.

245. Susan Flynn

246. Sadhguru

247. Susan Flynn

248. Susan Flynn

249. Unknown–healthline.com.

250. Susan Flynn

251. Susan Flynn

252- Katharine Hepburn–was an American actress and one of Hollywood's leading ladies, goodhousing.com.

253. Rob Hill Sr–known as the "heart healer," an actor and Navy veteran, pinterest.com.

254. Dodinsky–author, goodreads.com.

255. Susan Flynn

256. Susan Flynn

257. Najwa Zebian, goodreads.com.

258. Sylvester McNutt–eight- time best-selling author, speaker, and podcaster.

259. Alberto Casing– is known for his motivational words of wisdom quotes www.pinterest.com.

260. Ralph Marston–was a football player who spent a season in the National Football League.

261. Susan Flynn

262. Susan Flynn

263. Nikki Banas, author, small business owner of prints and other gifts.

264. Susan Flynn

265. Joel Osteen–American pastor and author, www.brainy-quote.com.

266. Ronald Reagan–America's 40th president from 1981 to 1989.

267. Janice Conklin–www.goodreads.com.

268- Zig Ziglar–was an American author and motivational speaker.

269. Miranda Marrott, www.goodreads.com.

270. Susan Flynn

271. Tupac Shakur–was an American rapper and actor.

272. Mandy Hale–blogger turned into a New York Times best-selling author.

273. Roger Lee– was the co-founder and president of NetMarket, Roger also co-found Corio.

274. Susan Flynn

275. Amy Weatherly–author, www.pinterest.com.

276. Charlie Remiggio–www.goodreads.com.

277. Susan Flynn

278. Charles Dickson–was an English writer and social critic, brainyquote.com.

279. Susan Flynn

280. Karen Salmansohn–self-help book author, goodreads.com.

281. George Washington–was an American military officer, statesman, and the founding father who served as the first US president from 1789 to 1797.

282. Susan Flynn

283. Susan Flynn

284. Epictetus–Greek Stoic.

285. Sunflower Gardener, pinterest.com.

286. Jimmy Osborne–country singer, songwriter.

287. Susan Flynn

288. Susan Flynn

289. Ziad K Abdelnour–Lebanese-born American financial advisor and author.

290. Wayne Dyer–was an American self-help author and motivational speaker.

291. Susan Flynn

292. Susan Flynn

293. Dodinsky–New York Times best-selling author.

294. Buddha–tinybuddha.com.

295. Susan Flynn

296. Susan Flynn

297. Susan Flynn

298. Nancy Hoffman–www.pinterest.com.

299. Susan Flynn

300. Allison Aars– is a mom www.quotespedia.org.

301. Susan Flynn

302. Alan Cohen–an author of twenty-seven popular inspi-rational books, including *The Dragon Doesn't Live Here Anymore* and *A Deep of Life.*

303. Susan Flynn

304. Susan Flynn

305. Susan Flynn

306. Hailey Williams–American singer, songwriter, and businesswoman.

307. Bianca Sparacino–is a Canadian author and podcaster, goodreads.com.

308. Bianca Sparacino–author.

309. Buddha–tinybuddha.com.

310. Susan Flynn

311. Susan Flynn

312. Mandy Hale–goodreads.com.

313. Amy Weatherly–goodreads.com.

314. Susan Flynn

315. Susan Flynn

316. John Wooden–was an American basketball coach and player. He won ten national collegiate athletics in a twelve-year period.

317. Davis Willis–is a journalist and broadcaster. He spent more than fifteen years as a foreign correspondent.

318. Marvin J Ashton– goodreads.com.

319. Susan Flynn

320. Susan Flynn

321. Susan Flynn

322. Susan Flynn

323. Susan Flynn

324. Jimmy Osborne–country singer-songwriter.

325. Susan Flynn

326. Susan Flynn

327. Susa Flynn

328. Susan Flynn

329. Susan Flynn

330. Dr. Abdul Kalam–was an Indian aerospace scientist who served as the 11th president of India from 2002 to 2007.

CPSIA information can be obtained
at www.ICGtesting.com
Printed in the USA
BVHW020947160922
647225BV00019B/419